D1082649

Imperfect Tense

MELISA CAHNMANN-TAYLOR

POEMS

Imperfect Tense

WHITEPOINT PRESS
SAN PEDRO, CALIFORNIA

Copyright © 2016 Melisa Cahnmann-Taylor
All rights reserved.

Except for brief quotations in critical articles or
reviews, no part of this book may be reproduced in any manner
without prior written permission from the publisher:
editors@whitepointpress.com

A Whitepoint Press First Edition 2016
Cover and book design by Monique Carbajal
Cover image © iStock.com/ivanastar

Author photo by Jason Thrasher

ISBN - 13: 978-1-944856-00-7
ISBN - 10: 1-944856-00-5

Library of Congress Control Number: 2016930863

Published by Whitepoint Press
whitepointpress.com

In memory of the most beloved
and imperfect champion of this work,
Bertha Shraer
November 18, 1923 - March 20, 2015

... Contents ...

II. Past Tense

III. EVER PRESENT TENSE

I
IMPERFECT TENSE

Whorfian Hypothesis

I wouldn't have thought "rice particles"
until reading them, unconditionally named,

      subtitled from Tagalog,

or of measuring, as Cambodians do,
the length from elbow to tip of middle finger.

      Any number of words   *"builds a house of consciousness."*

One rock [ahsin] in Ojibwe contains
bald eagle spirit just as *"la"* in *"la roca"* houses gender,

and to say *"babka"* in Polish is to link "grandmother"
with the loaf served at Easter,

      counted differently from a Japanese slice.

Our idioms order *he* (third person, singular male subject)
before *drives* (verb) and *her* (the object) up

an inanimate *wall* whose blue chipped hue
can only be described in New Guinea

      as either *"dark"* or *"cold."*

Few of us learn to count in the language of mantis shrimps,
whose eyes see in 12 primary colors to our three,

linguistic systems of sight where whole spectrums go untranslated.

I'd like to lift the blinds, feel my blood stir as it once did,
catching faraway nouns by the tail.

WHEN YOU'RE A RETIRED AMERICAN STUDYING SPANISH IN MEXICO AND AFTER SIX MONTHS CAN BARELY ORDER SOMETHING OFF A MENU

Chances are you've said *I'm pregnant* when you meant

    I'm embarrassed,
                fuck a bus

    when you wanted   to *catch it,*

or *vaginas*

    instead of "páginas"   to describe an art book's pages.

Odds are you've boozed these errors,

    loosened   the alveolar ridge,

    that ineffable   tongue flap

that probably made all the difference

when you lacked that packed *poncho,*

    exact *pesos*

        or translations for the dose, the punch line,

the bus route,   the landlord,   the speedy

vowels garbled into the phone you answered and fat

      chance you sent   the right words back,

      misreading ingredients,

hunting for ATMs.   Filthy footed, fed

up with it all, you tangled in a carnival of outlets,

      sickened from taco   cilantro,

      broke   human likenesses

with a stick.   You risked   time

reduced to   mere   numerals,

      a few verbs   that evaporated

      like desert water.   Raw

as the bed-frame wood that men
          back-holstered up missing cobblestones,

you startled like   patron saint firecrackers

      outside   a sleepy weeknight

      wooden door.   But when you creaked,

      wide-awake, to blue mornings,   you exposed

like a rare   book's ink sensitive pages, as if damage

mattered   less to you than a small, braided fist of cheese.

Whey spilt, you inevitably unraveled,   turned question marks
        upside down until tart tamarind   tasted sweet.

WIDOWED NYC TEACHER STUDIES GRAMMAR IN MEXICO

Imperfect means

> incomplete, a bruised
> pear reduced
> in price, a cat
> who *purred* for hours
> while 501 verbs surfed
> conjugations, continuous
> waves of what was, what used
> to be, what no longer exists.

Te amaba, me amabas, nos amabamos

> Not a map's stickpin to
> Brooklyn, more highlighter
> glide across an open workbook's
> spine, *pesos* doled out
> *per diem* like guilt
> from a *pishke*
> *cup*, pouring ever-
> present rain.

I was working. I used to be married.

> Describe perfect's
> opposite:
> a house cramped
> with winter rooms,

fractured bones
percolating in
widowed franchises
until Spanish classes
sparked a pretense
of purpose:

reir [to laugh]; reíamos [we used to laugh],

She began with habitual
error, unceasing
fault: She
used to correct
high school
English—*I been,
you been*—until
she'd been
burned, bored,
bordered on sub-par,
parsing sense.
Now, she chooses
what to edit, attends
to contextual cues:

siempre, con frequencia, a veces, todos los días

usually the imperfect
follows, no—
she says, it always does.

First Grade

In dedication to Maxine Kumin

Two thousand three hundred nine words
rhyme with "*estar*" but my son can't think
of any for his *tarea en español*, prefers
action figure distractions, spilling his drink,

breaking pencils, falling from his chair—
anything that's *not* homework until
I offer "*vomitar*," to vomit and "*estornudar*"
to sneeze. Pleased, he asks if "to kill"

in Spanish would rhyme, and "to hit," and "fart,"
—smart boy, figuring out a second tongue
multiplies words that disconcert, courts
deep laughter in dark theatres. So strong

his will to be liked, to understand peers, offer
jokes, to translate "butt" and savor what comes after.

FRIJOLERO EX-PATS

Pancita soup, *tasajo,*
    chuletas de cerdo, they
search pocket dictionaries
    for cuts of meat, eat

oxtail and tripe with *pan casero*
    (Oh! *homemade!*). Beans
baked in clay pots for days.
    "Gringos," sure, but mostly

they find the people kind,
    despite the "white" effect: this
means more costly taxi rides
    but at times more respect. Old

people here treated with *dignidad,*
    the more grey or yellow,
the more *"express"* their cards.
    This aging pair

in brand-new rugged pants,
    prance backpacked to dinner,
haggle rugs made by hand.
    "*Casero?*" Is

this the word? No: *Hecho a mano.*
    The price: absurd! A
gendered mistake *(¿el mano?)*, verbs
    imperfectly tensed, their casual

errors make formal requests.
    Snowbirds in Mexico, no affair
for the fearful or frail. Pepto-Bismol,
    probiotics, and plain

water in *talavera*, or in hand blown
    glass, *flan* on chipware
laced with lead. On Days of the Dead,
    why not dine on

green glazes? Free health care,
    cheap meds, a
doctor not needed, even
    Viagra pills in plain

white boxes at half their
    American price. And
playa resorts off season
    rejuvenate creaking

joints. They adapt backs
    to box springs of wood,
loom walls with fabric or
    ornaments pressed from tin,

all lightweight,
    then packed flat
    into bags checked to where
they March home.

In Mexico, Americans Struggle

With *guayaberas*
  that don't fit their torsos;
    keys to front doors;

dust; patience; ordering
  pizza con pepperoni by phone;
    declining hand-painted toothpicks;

the "blonde effect" —*no one*
  thinks I speak Spanish; "morena," and
    everyone thinks I know

more than I do; people
  who correct; people
    who don't

break things   down:
  "to ask"—*pedir* or *preguntar*?
    "to know"—*saber* or *conocer*?

Are they *bien or bueno*?
  When to use the subjunctive?
    Ser or *Estar*?

Many misunderstand their gardeners,
  waiters, children, cleaning ladies;
    some of them stutter,

arrive too early; only a few

detest flan, depressed by
  elisions—*pa'lante* they say

but is it "*por*" or "*para*," forward or back?
  The kissing thing's hard—mothers
    order handsome sons

to greet women this way.
  Of the ones who stay, most say
    they get used to it.

Medical Professional Says, "I Would Prefer to Go to Sleep"

I always loved words, especially French and Italian—they sound
so *sexy*. I love the mystery, it's like "Oh? Is that a silent letter?"
Whereas, Spanish, it just doesn't DO it for me. Then I got fired, some
whistleblower thing and I thought: "Okay, now I HAVE to learn
Spanish." The whole conjugation thing is like, *wait*. What? I struggle
with indirect pronouns, *that which*, and all that's in my spreadsheets:
infinitives I don't need.—*ar* verbs, *-ir*, *-er*, reflexives. I flash cards and
my brain scrambles. I hunker with post-traumatic disorder; I keep
getting triggered, you know, by childhood. The teacher asked, "What
was *bonito*?" and I'm like NOTHING! I cry in class. I just want the
past tense, "es" words that start with "s" in English, "shun" words,
subtle changes in pronunciation, *pro-nun-cia-ción*. But how do you
make Spanish fun when it's a means to an end?

Iberian Chair 1840s, Decorative Arts Collection

Say *chair* and feel abstraction's weight,
    not classic mission, fabric,
    or rattan cane, not head or director,
but this decorative art unmoored

from its coupling: rocking___, electric ___.
    Hear its strained, *cherry*
    purpose, scuffed loosening
from rooms, as if *ch* might fall, leaving *air*

stacked in broken corners. Tilt
    it to *cheer* and clink glasses
    while the meat *chars*, left too long
by the sitter, the soldier, the rocker,

the curator, the one who certifies
    preservation and forbids
    touch.   Survivor of the War
of Jenkin's Ear, this wooden Spaniard

is severed, too, from use, a stretched
    rawhide reminder, shrunk to sit out
    dispute. *See ya*, one might say
in its native tongue and we do

not sit on *la silla*, we don't recline
    in others' tongues because we won
    an ordinary household article,
our museums tell us so.

Anika Says, "We Are Eternal"

French gets easier. Kiswahili gets easier. I don't think that way about Spanish. It gets more challenging. I manage the tenses, but it's the massive amount of nouns and adjectives. A lot of words aren't even in Spanish! *Tlaxcala* and *Quetzalcoatl*—Aztec words blended in! English is extremely open and welcoming. You can speak English any kind of way, and nobody's gonna say anything to you. What other people bring to English gets adopted, sort of like the Borg in *Star Trek*. We have English words because of cultural, what do you call it? Appropriation? Spanish isn't like that. French isn't like that at all, and in a few hundred years, I just feel that French will be dead! I had one woman tell me, "just think in Spanish." That makes no sense. How do you get up in the morning and start thinking about your day in Spanish when you don't have vocabulary? When I leave Mexico, that's it for Spanish. You know, like the everyday constant interaction: going to the *mercado* or to the store, you know, going to see a movie or to a club, ordering drinks. It's done when I leave here. This slows me down in becoming proficient, but I can accept that. We are eternal. And who knows, in two years I may decide I want to go to Croatia, or maybe to West Africa or Senegal, or Benin, where they speak French.

Sarah's Advice: Find Someone to Talk to and Pay Them

Before we came to Oaxaca I took classes at Baruch College in New York, but I didn't do very well. I NEVER did my homework which is my M.O.—that's Latin, now I remember THAT! Anyhow, I'd show up for class, do the best I could. But now, six years of living here in Mexico full time, I feel I've a really good understanding of Spanish. I can listen to people and generally understand them perfectly. I mean, get the gist. Sometimes it depends who's speaking. Mostly, I just glaze over trying to figure out what they're saying. When I started my goal was to *kibbitz*, get my needs met and I've definitely accomplished that. Now, my goal's to express more, beyond chatting with the cab driver. So the last couple of months I've been walking with a young man whose first language is Spanish and who knows English. And I'm multi-tasking! Walking my dog and talking conversational Spanish with Fernando! Two hours, totally in Spanish! It's opened me up to express myself, to tell a whole story. Friday I spent almost two hours describing a documentary I'd seen. The concepts were complicated and to do it all in Spanish—that was a miracle! And I'm proud of myself. I'm moved. Now this is going to get psychological but having success, I never imagined it! I have a tendency to put myself down, that I'm not very good at certain things. I'm normally saying I should be better. I'm here six years and I should know more. I'd like to speak without struggling so much, get a handle of certain very basic words like "to see" and "to hear." I can't conjugate them and I'd like to have the "*-abas*" and "*-ibas*"—the imperfect is so good for telling stories.

Warner Says, "A Great Place for Black People"

When I got to Morehouse in Atlanta, you had to take up to level four in Spanish. And I just said, you know what? I can't do this. But I had to. I said, listen I'm just gonna figure out some way to survive, cheat my way through. Then these two students had just gotten back from the Dominican Republic and they spoke to my class—two black guys who looked just like me going back in forth between English and Spanish. Something about seeing those two folks being able to do that, and I just said, you know what? I gotta figure this out! This was pre-internet and it was only what you could see in the *Encyclopedia Britannica*. So I looked up the Dominican. They had a picture of a man in the sugar cane fields with a machete, and I said, "Well, I'm not going there!" When you grow up lower middle class, or "high class poor," whatever you want to call it, you don't volunteer for any suffering. So I went to Madrid, a big city where African immigrants are looked down upon. They don't walk up to black people randomly and say "Hey, where you from?" One day I looked up and it was like: I'm broke, my Spanish is not advancing the way I would've thought, I'm hungry. You know, am I gonna spring for this little *tortilla española* or am I just gonna drink some water for dinner? That's how I ended up in Mexico. They just walk up to you all the time and have conversations with you. I felt rich! I could eat all the tacos I wanted! I ended up coming back to Oaxaca every summer for 19 years and then I moved here. I first went to the university to see what's up and I saw this group of guys watching NBA highlight videos. It was like Michael Jordan's hey day. When I peeked my head in the door everybody was like COME IN COME IN COME IN COME IN!!!!! I love this place. It's a great place for Black people to be.

JESSIE SAYS, "MEXICANS ARE RACIST…BUT INTERCAMBIOS ARE GREAT"

After my children left, I wanted to create my life anew. I wanted a language. Every place you go in the US now, things are in Spanish. So, I said okay, Spanish is what it will be. In 2008 my then-husband and my children gave me a trip, you know to Oaxaca, to do a weaving workshop in Teotítlan for my birthday. This was a month after my ex-husband had asked for a divorce, so when I came to Mexico, I was feeling pretty bad. But something just told me that this just might be what I'd been needing. I kept coming back and by 2011 I'd met this really good friend and she said: classes are good but, it's really good to do *intercambios* and just talk. But I've found Mexicans are very racist. They've got some color shit going on up here. I have a friend who's an attorney who I did my first *intercambio* with, and she's fair skinned, very fair, and the way she talks! Like when we go to a restaurant, the way she talks to the waiters and the waitresses! They're usually darker, and it seems like the darker they are the worse she talks to them! If I go to clubs, and there're White girls from the US, especially blonde girls, Mexican men go *crazy*. This is not to say that men should notice *me* —I'm not saying that. But if a guy comes up to me in a club packed full of Mexicans I know he must *really* want to talk to me. There are a lot of guys here that simply prefer foreign women. They find them exciting, interesting. My ex-husband is like that. But I think intercambios are great because I learn almost as much vocabulary and it's far more useful. I remember doing a lesson in my Spanish class about things in the kitchen, and committing things to memory. I remember using the word *lavaplatos*, and my friend *Perla* was like what is a *lavaplatos*? And I told her, "it's like a machine that washes the dishes," and she's like, "uh, we don't have those."

DOTTIE EXPLAINS HOW TO PRACTICE SPANISH IN THE UNITED STATES

There are service people who speak Spanish but it never occurs to me to speak with them. Is that weird or what? It's a mindset, you know? I'm afraid that when I meet someone who speaks Spanish that I'll speak to them and they'll fire back and I'll go, *uhhhhh, now I really don't speak Spanish.* Or I worry I'll offend someone. I worry some people are Latino but they were raised in the US and they don't speak Spanish. And it's really embarrassing if I try to speak with them. There are quite a number of Spanish people who live in Minneapolis but it's a certain area of the city where a lot of people don't feel comfortable. What I do, for example, is if I make a phone call and they say press 1 for English or "2" for Spanish or hold on or whatever, I hold on. Then I say to the person who answers, "*Perdón, estoy practicando mi español, por favor, me puedes ayudar? Porque quiero comprar un boleto* [Excuse me, I'm practicing my Spanish, can you help me? Because I want to buy a ticket]." It's good to speak to a Spanish speaker that way. Then they have lots of patience.

NICK'S MATTRESSES

When I started teaching math, I was 29 in East Harlem. All the kids
were Dominican. In the mornings the girls talked about *Mar y Mar*,
the soap opera. So, I started recording it. The girls would talk about
it and I would try to piece it together. I would watch it over and
over again. That was when I really started learning Spanish. I started
going two months in summer, two weeks at Passover to Barcelona. I
started chatting on Messenger for an apartment exchange. I bought
magazines and translated them. I'd read bilingual children's books.
I watched movies with subtitles. I've had fun looking up a word in
Spanish and reading all the comments. I've been vigorously teaching
myself. I like languages, I'm good at them, but Spanish helped me the
most. But after 20 years of vacations and even after two years living
full time in Mexico, I still don't see myself as native-like. Absolutely
not. In English, I'm a leader. I like to be a big shot, to be in charge.
But if I'm sitting with 8 people speaking Spanish, I cannot tell the
jokes. I cannot be the leader. I cannot be the organizer. I sound like
an idiot. I still write things down—these are the last few words I've
looked up. Okay *fulminante*, it's like if you have a sudden heart
attack, "all of a sudden." And *escamoso*. I saw that in a museum and
it means "scaly." *Abnegada*, that's like a "suffering mother." I went to
Home Depot with my friend and I found out *tarja* means kitchen
sink. I have to tell you something I did when I first came here. I
was staying with a friend and a truck would pass by every day going
badadabada dabadadaba dadabadada badadaba-da-da. And I said,
"What's he saying?" And my friend was like, "I don't know and I
don't care." So I tape recorded it with my Blackberry. I listened to it
a thousand times. A thousand, thousand times. I have severe OCD.
One day the guy came to the street and I understood! He was saying:
colchones, colchones, compramos colchones, colchones usadas, colchones

manchadas, colchones que no te sirve. He was buying and selling mattresses! I was so happy. I want to understand everything they're saying. That's the kind of person I am. That's why my Spanish is so good.

II
PAST TENSE

Teaching Poetry in Georgia Schools

My house is like a pond, she says. *Is so pretty.*
    I ask her to say it again.
        Can you say that again?
            Did you say "pond"?

Round body of water behind a Vermont house
    where a white girl skinny dips and geese
        make merry with picnics:
            How can a house be like a pond?

She tells me Grandmom bakes custard pies,
    green carpets the kitchen,
        her daddy cooks candy, a waterfall's by the door.
        I ask her to say it again.

Can you say that again?
    Did you say "waterfall by the door"?

I don't know if water rivers by her house,
    a cheap frame splashes a flea market image,
        or a neighbor's pipes flush through the wall.
            She writes about rainbows, spells rain *rian* and *bow*

as a separate word and *door* with two r's and one o
    and she sits next to a boy who prints he's from *Mixeco*.
        Her skin colors like pine bark; her eyes, behind small
            gold frames, pond with life made visible

through close looking. I know this school trailer,
but I'm from a house like a jewel box.
She asks me to say it again.

Can you say it again?
Did you say "jewel box?" Tha's nice.

Driving through North Philly

—September, 1998

I meet the shoes on Eighth Street
—must be thirty pair perched upside down,
an uneven silhouette of sneakers
slung over electric wire; the lightness
soaked out, except from eager cleats,
less familiar with whims of weather.

Here a boy doesn't give up shoes
unless they give up on him;
he bruises like September leaves,
and measures kicks through corn chip bags
crushed in the city's side-pockets.

I imagine reasons for these pairs in flight:
maybe to test gravity, feet got too big,
or a protest, like tilting chairs and
gouging desktop names instead of
on time, straight, school-yard lines.

For weeks I wonder until I stop
to ask a neighborhood kid, a black boy,
backpack over left shoulder, pants big enough
for two of him. He studies me, a white woman
with notepad and loopy earrings.

"Because it's fun, Miss,"
as if he sprayed the answer
in oversized bubble letters.
And then, "So they remember you when you're gone."

I've lived in thirteen apartments
over the last nine years and I've never left anything behind.
I look at the newest pair, think how
the color fades, perfectly good and out of reach,
an empty walk on sky.

"I done it lotsa times, Miss," he grins.
How little I must know about this joy,
what it's like to throw something up in the air
that's important, that weighs something, that takes you places—
and not wait for it to come down.

INTERNATIONAL STUDENT HAS A QUESTION AFTER POETRY CLASS

for Echo

You know I broke my knee
in class last week, she says. *Scraped,*

I correct, *not broke.* I'd fussed
over the red-orange Georgia

sassafras in her poem compared
to Tianjin's more yellowed

ashes. Then she'd un-
balanced, carpeted after praise.

This week she hesitates,
then pulls the bandage, asks

advice because the sore's
still moist, puckered, her

roommate's worried.
Suddenly, she's my five

year old daughter, wincing
as I dab cotton to peroxide,

foaming the scrape's inevitable
blood, the itchy, salted

healing. *You'll be fine,*
I assure before registering

litigations, then encourage
a health center visit

to confirm the wound's
not infected. But I wouldn't go.

I'd just observe
the scab's darkening

parts, editing the skin's
new grammar underneath.

Kuo's First Attempt

So nervous I almost forget key
to my boyfriend car. He know best
way to get there on Chinese

time: early. Wait room still full, at least
10 American in line at DDS
I so nervous, I almost forget key

on plastic chair. My boyfriend tease
me, say I forget right from left
way, urge me think in Chinese

all steps before say hello to White Lady.
She famous on immigrant blog, detest
foreigners. I so nervous, forget turn key

for ignition. I look boyfriend way, freeze
when she say *blinker* or *braker*, I make guess
to move. Boyfriend in backseat whisper Chinese

word. *You fail!* she say. *You learn for speak
English first!* She not even give chance to pass
test. So nervous, I almost forget key
rule on U.S. road: don't speak Chinese.

Undocumented Youth March for In-State Tuition

You didn't bathe in our hospital registration lights or nurse
    in our fluoride waters.

You, whose refrigerated parents slit our chickens' wings,
    trim our dirtiest windows, wipe our snottiest children,
    deliver our cheap muffins and exclusive auto parts,

You, we pronounce, do not deserve to study here.

You who've learned to speak "our" language, you who believed
    our gospel of Standardized Test.

You've won! *Good Citizen Award* in third grade; *Attendance Award*,
    fifth grade; *Leadership Award*, tenth grade.

You who didn't drop out or dope up or unleash the tiger of anger;

You who didn't let prejudice's anvil crush your brown heart or "anchor
    baby" sink your forward motion cargo;

You skipped a senior day in high school to march at this institution
    which banishes you from its arches, not for who you *are*
    but for who you are not.

You whose anthems remind us that *todos somos immigrantes*, you
   already know this isn't about *you*,
   but how we've over-drafted,
   how our weapons need both bullets and targets,
   and how we're afraid—that you

full speed ahead, without papers or license, may accidentally forget to stop.

YOU RECEIVE A PRESENT FROM SOMEONE YOU HAVEN'T SEEN IN A LONG TIME. WHO'S IT FROM? WHAT'S INSIDE?

—Writing prompt at Jubilee Partners ESOL Program for Refugees, Comer, GA.

This Congolese boy describes hide and seek with a twist. The Finder
must shoot the Found with a "to-PI-co." I draw the sling's "Y" shot,
and we review adjectives: *playful, violent.* They use seeds, not rocks.
He swears it's not a violent game he's missing with his friends. Maybe
just the culture of boys playing. Already a man at 17, mothered by his
sister while the split family grieves over a sibling's typhoid, a missing
father. A mother in Texas grieves. She let her boy play with neighbors
whose chambers held loaded handguns. The yellow tape. The no
return. She preaches we ask before sending children on playdates to
unsafe houses. Foam swords. Squirt guns. Games that allow the player
to spell *bomb* so one appears and blows holes through a virtual wall.
A boy-almost-a-man, 21, rented our house while we lived in Mexico.
I didn't know he hunted. He demanded his full deposit though he'd
punched a hole through my son's door. *I patched it*, he argued. *It
better be good enough.* Slight threat as he insisted I search for lost
fishing hooks. It's better to withdraw where there are bullets. But
what do you do when your village is burned? Do you get the deposit
back? Do you offer a limb? A daughter or son? While one remembers
a war-toy, another girl conjures a pair of green shoes. Imagination's
tucked into every child like a hidden coin or buried like a sandbox in
concrete. This boy has 2 months before he's to pay rent, find a job,

buy his own shoes in this confusing and green country. The Christian
volunteers were to bury a death row inmate and the Salvadorans
insisted they'd shovel better. Unable to bury their own, they moved
earth for our discarded men. *Éste por mi mama. Éste por mi papa.*
They slung red clay in the rhythms of a clapping game.

A Taste of War

—June, 2006

We watch the World Cup in Bozîca's village—Croatia down
1-0. Red and white checkered hats droop because, as her cousin

groaned, *this country deserves a tie.* We devour links of pork,
mounds of fried lamb with bread. Civil war started on this border.

Fifteen years later men crowd around outdoor television sets
while women in church courtyards dance. *After the war we work*

for Red Cross. Serbs, Croats, everyone. We have to work.
There is much anger. Bozîca smokes like a movie star. I want her

to tell my new husband and me what she learned when forced to flee
a burning house. I only know about missed ferries and burnt

toast. I'd paid to see museum photographs, fifty *kuna* to walk
the ancient port city's fortress, shoot pictures where arrows

pierced Turks. Now windows open onto barefoot boys
playing soccer, cherry gelato for sale. We drove to this border

to hike Croatia's parks, lodge where grasses and small
trees recovered, but what do the old women remember, selling

spheres of cheese, honey, strudel? Pines can't help but grow back.
So good, the Red Cross took care of them: murderers, mothers, all.

Abundance of lavender, fish, ache. Our hostess offers brandy
and lessons in good-bye, the syrup so sweet I can hardly taste it.

DRAGON FRUIT

Among the milder cousins' familiar suits—
bananas sewn in yellow or packaged plastic
bags of Bartlett pears—lay these fresh recruits

from faraway lands. Hot pink, fantastic
leathery skins. Like mail order brides just landed,
they surprise: exposed yet overdressed, drastic

difference in taste and tint, stranded
and browning alongside small baskets
of spikey-haired *rambutan*, *lychee*, five-handed

star fruit. This daring, misplaced mascot
of beauty might be savored in Thailand
or closer in Mexican *mercados*, bought

for its black-dotted, mildly sweet flesh. "*Pitaya*,"
Yucatán whisper turned alien traveler, grocery
oddity. Better a navel orange, Walmart shoppers

think, passing this exotic court. Such royalty
a small child notices, perched like a *quetzal*
at the shopping cart's front. *Mommy, mommy,*

I want THAT one! The spikey pink turtle!
Mother's distracted, selects a Liberty apple.

Ghetto Teachers' Apology

I'm afraid, sweet Wilmarie, we've lied.
We didn't teach you how to hide

your Rite Aid salary from Wel-
fare in a Dominican bank. We didn't tell

you how to find a roommate or put a lock
on your bedroom door or how to walk

after sundown by yourself, slouch
at your brother's funeral, patch

bullet holes in an open casket in your living room.
We never told you,

like your boss, you can't speak English,
or like your cousin, you can't speak Spanish.

We didn't tell you how to live on
$5.50 an hour or that at seven-

teen you'd be an orphan. We didn't want to sour
our hopes and fictions, we wanted you to flower,

and prove us wrong. Sweet Wilmarie,
we're sorry.

We didn't live on your side of town
between crack houses and crackdowns.

We're not like you, we didn't know how to survive
behind shatter proof glass with those pretty brown eyes.

In Silence

A bug flew into my right cornea so the doctor asked me
to cover the left and read sideways prongs. I guessed
"E" but second guessed "F" or "I." With the foreign object
blurring sight I didn't know what to expect from signs

anymore, like the balloon-tied one between the parking lot
and University. When I saw Black girls clustered
on concrete steps, round streetlamps of hair atop young
bodies, I guessed minority recruitment until I parked

and walked closer to "Blood Drive." The drops dimmed
sight of the tallest among them. She might have sat comfortably
on nothing, like Marcel Marceau trapped inside a cage made
by his own gloved hands. I walked inside my white-faced

world where I rested on a chair's edge pulled out
from under me. Yet, I sat still, white gloves crossed
over absurdist knee, thighs burning to create the front row's
illusion. These girls might have been waiting

for class, wanting to give. I didn't ask.

Pinewood Estates Trailer Park

Adriana
Leo
Yellow Shirt
Dinosaur Boy

We talk gum-stuck
shoes, fuzzy chicks, the movie
screens in our minds
when I play *Billie Jean*
or *Miss Thang*, to write
without scratch-outs or look
backs or do overs or I can'ts
but from shivers and loves
like Yellow Shirt who comes
late, and leaves
the after-school library trailer
to show his mother
his poem.

Angel
Orlando
Mariela
Martín

Angel messed up. Yéssica
didn't share. Dinosaur boy
wrote about Tyrannosaurus
Rex. Martín wrote every word
that went with "baby brother":
stroller, baby carrier, fever, crib.

Yéssica
Wilfredo
Ana
Gabriel

We read "What Moms
and Dads do" poems
and they write how some Dads speed
and get sent back to México,
some do cocaine
and *I knew a boy once*
who had white stuff coming out
his nose and mouth and he died,
and *Grass, some smoke that,*
a seven-year-old raises
an invisible joint to lips. *Not*
my dad, says Yéssica,
but some Dads
do.

Marta
Alejandro
Sandra
Guillermo

They list gasoline on Dad's hands,
Dad's big muscles shoveling dirt, a Dad
reading dinosaurs with his son.
Leo has glasses. He doesn't
stop writing. He wins
candy for coming. He leaves
behind his poem.

GEORGIA HORIZONTAL

Americans love walls.
          Mine aren't thick enough to block
the neighbor's lonely-for-some-girl
                    songs or the trash truck's
backward squawks.
          The Army-Navy school trespasses
yards with trumpets like the tree swallows'
                              liquid chirping.

*

I save a trash bag of clothes for the Salvadoran
          cleaning woman and her nest
of migrant cousins. They seem glad
                    for old jerseys, neckties, my ex's
old mattress
          until I say they can blow them up
for all I care, and startle
                    by how we throw out words
          and television sets in this country.

*

Tea breath rises in grey air. Black birds'
          subdued calls rumor in bare branches.
The realtor says to redecorate the garden,
                              something showy,
like pink hydrangeas.
          The girlfriend next door blocks

the mailbox, my "For Sale" sign.
    Face over an empty mug, I miss
        the steam's vanished comfort.

        *

The birds choose one tree to throw
        a party, loud and congested as a Northeastern city.
    Falling black stars zip across, down. Groups
          on a mission
to buy more beer, or plot terror:
        the remaining swarm
    ready to eat a house or several.

        *

They're cowbirds, the avian
        equivalent to kudzu, exploiting others' nests and eggs,
          their tense descent
        dropping pecans onto tin roofs
like bullets. Weed birds, unhappy adolescents. Uneasy
        with nature I'd once thought beautiful,
before I knew dandelions were blemishes or my colleague
divorced. I thought she had pink eye.
Now, I'm getting married.
        What if joy turns greedy for seed?

        *

Rain falls like old bread,
    chiss, chiss
    on the street's skillet.

How to leave this house—
the speckled cordial glass cracked,
   but I registered for a dozen more.
  How we'll live together: trash cans
 huddled curbside like refugees, rituals
     shelved like books
on yawning, empty mouths.
      Alone time, sports time, horizontal time.
  Ice melts with a regular
    ping of water.

    *

Southern transplant, I learned the garden's
    names on red clay knees,
  planting a bag of bulbs. Now,
     Sundays, I join the unenlisted who trim lawns,
too old to learn to kill with our hands. This year
    daffodils bloom early, duped by a few days
  of misplaced   spring.

    *

Planning to lose may seem unnatural, soothes
    the Realignment and Closure Commission.
     There's always more to throw away:
  cotton balls, military bases, looks, words.
A yellow bus removes our neighborhood children,
     a harbinger of futures in foreign deserts,
     absence from their Georgia bases—
thirteen of them, but the Navy School will close soon.

Two Moons over Tel Aviv

I have special glasses, he says.
I can see two moons.

They walk the tideline and can't see the medusas,
though they're there. Vaseline jellyfish bodies
spread like hubcaps on cold sand, washed up
with condoms and plastic Israeli flags.

He's an ill-fit for her heart caught like a shoe
in the deep brown pocket sand makes
when water draws out to sea.

They walk hand-in-hand anyhow, as if the sweepers had come
and the beach were new and all the earth and sky
could begin again, swept of doll parts,
broken glass.

A fat crescent splits into a thin double.
They have two moons. He's given one to her.
It comes on a small wave when her back turns,
pushes her toward shore.

Mordechai Sheftall's Letter to His Mother, 1812
Savannah, GA

There's nothing to fear, *Sheyna Mamele*. To tighten
tefillin's noose, binds us to Tragedy's

past. Our duty now to loose ourselves to coastal
winds, escape *halachah's* dictates and flush Yiddish

tongues with English fresh waters. This soil
welcomes Jews, heathen, dissenters, laboring

minds that market collective goods. Here, they'll beat
bigotry's spoiled grapes into vineyards, hate's

moth-like wings into silken prosperity. Celebrate
my marriage to the Reverend's daughter, and aim

to convert such 'Old Country' visions of loss
to fertile apple and honey fields. Is the Swallowtail

not destiny for a caterpillar child? *Ve-Ahabta*
eth Adonai Elohecha—your prayer which commands

door posts bear signs of our difference yet
cleaves Ashkenazi from Sephardi cousin,

cuts us from Protestant and Catholic brothers as cotton
hulls rip slave flesh. Don't grip what you can't hold, Dear

Mother. Survival's a trade: deerskin for another's hide.

1750, NATURAL HISTORY OF BARBADOS IN TEN BOOKS, RUSSELL SPECIAL COLLECTIONS

Each fragile and leather-bound book documents the island: Air, Soil, Climate; Diseases; Animals, Reptiles, Insects; Trees, Shrubs, Plants. Book X treats Sea Fishes.

Such as have not at all or imperfectly been described before.

Reverend Hughes described "The Mud Fish," and its "Small Fins, *post Bronchia*, under the gullet." The entry, *The Sharks* on page 312, cautioned from dated experience.

These Creatures are sometimes very numerous among the
Ships of Carlisle-Bay; especially when there are many
Vessels with Slaves crouded (sic) together in one Bottom,

Vessels, Slaves, Bottom, haphazard capitalization of the Containers and the Contained; the writer's crude distinction between the lower and upper cases.

a great many of them die with various Diseases; bring
together a Multitude of these voracious Animals,

Diseases, Multitude, Animals. It's difficult to read the archaic font sprouting "f" from "s," to grasp the warning.

that it is not

"safe" spelled "fafe" so I read "sase" and "fase" until I understand *not*

safe at such Times for the fatigued Sailors to refresh
themselves by bathing in the Bay.

This was not irony. This fear of sharing the same water, not Dickie
B. or Strom Thurmond and Dixiecrat platitudes about the pool. This
was not Michael Brown, Tamir Rice, Eric Garner, Trayvon Martin.
This is deep and vaulted and stored in dry, 50 degree air. Catalogues
and ledgers, maps and manuscripts. Discomfort. Laughter. This
question she secreted on a raft down the Broad River, buckled to a life
vest.

> *Do you mind if I tell a racist joke?*

This vulgar language. This common ghost. This rare book. These
sour flags. This marble house, this granite, this Bottom we threw
overboard, this archive, this other warning:

> *Do not move suddenly. Do not run. Keep hands where they*
> *can be seen. Be cordial. Be polite. Never ask questions.*
> *Never match outfits. More than three dressed in the same color*
> *equals a gang.*

The Sharks. A group is called a *gam, a herd, a school, a shiver.*

WOMAN SHOWS ME WHERE WE ARE
IN THE SERVICE

I ate the candy. I didn't know
gum pellets and taffy arrows were meant
to be thrown at the Bar Mitzvah boy
who ducked behind the *bema.*

I was already sucking. Hard
watermelon stuck to my teeth when she
recited laws of prohibition and abstinence
where it is also written:

A boy entering manhood
with braces and two-toned hair
will pass out candy   You   Shall   Abominate
before winged creatures sting the flesh of a twelve-year old
in the presence of the   Lord   Your   God

Then you shall partake in perpetuity without suffering.
Then you shall be called out "Clean! Clean!"
Ancestors will do your laundry.
You will eat from the Kingdom of Confection.

In the second row of the synagogue of our confinement
I thought I was good. I had my finger
pressed on the right page in the book, I knew
when to sit and when to stand and with whom

to lie down and fuck after the Bar Mitzvah until
the sweet in my cheek gave me away

to the woman sitting next to me who
gave me a piece of her candy,

so I'd have something to throw.

The Cantor in Drag on Yom Kippur

No one knows I stole the blue velvet pouch
when he died. The white shawl lay inside, stained
spit yellow like aged teeth. I never expected

to wear it, a waste to have kept it so long
in the same drawer as panties and brassieres.
What would he think of me as Cantor?

Kissing four corners, pounding my chest
with a flapper's fringe, a finger latched to hem,
pointing toward God's book where the commandment is written

to atone, to mourn
a china cabinet filled with *kiddish* cups, one
for each son. I took one of those too,

and the vessel still sits broken on my kitchen counter
to remind me what a broken world I am, borrowing
books and cups and taking

what should not belong to me. As a girl
I sat at his table and wished for the hum of words
to stop, and the little water cup

to wash away hands. His propped feet
on a torn footstool stuffed with discarded
women's stockings. Grandfather,

you and your hunched back and angry
reminders to return *Of Mice
and Men* to the shelf. Here I am

in wrinkled blue and white polyester.
The rough hemline settles at the back of my neck
like a hand resting there, as I sing.

DEAD SEA VACATION

They say to be careful
with preformed beings who cook

in hot water, better to wait
until pieces of finger and eye

mix with melon in market
explosions. Pregnant, she rides buses,

opens satchels to girls in fatigues
carrying AK-47s. *Blame it*

on the Jews. Those Jews, the Jewish artist says,
the one who broke bread with the most hard-boiled

enemies. Does the woman's fetus
know the heat he steps into? Humans,

the only creatures to adapt to salt
and death, float like corks on holiday.

A mother of five from the Lebanese border
labored leg after leg to the salty pool:

You never get used to it, nu?

Krakow

A friend clicks through salt mine pictures,
storybook rooftops, beet soup,

pierogis by the dozen. Such a deal
traveling there, bed and breakfasts less

than half what it would cost to visit slave
plantations in Charleston, half the time

and airfare to resorts near India's
brothels. From the gate he captured

barrack snapshots, tourist lines
waiting to be refused

cameras inside. His return flight
stopped in London where he marched

with British protestors bearing signs, "We're all
Hezbollah." Admission free:

London's National Gallery, Auschwitz.
I asked him to tell me again, how much

one pays for fried lard, sour rye soup? How much
to visit the graves, what's left of the shallow,

salty, underground sea?

1971 Traveler's Guide to Jewish Landmarks of Europe

A women's ritual bath addressed at the ghetto's edge on Judenbadgasse
(Jews' Bath Street) survived because stones stepped underground to
dressing rooms and pool. Women humidified Dubrovnik sinuses.
What a big nose you have! Remarked the old Hungarian in Budapest
near the statue of the great Baron who freed Jews in 1867 to smell
anything they wanted. Rhinoplasty hadn't been invented, and
enemies had already stolen baskets of heirlooms. Visitors jubilate
the living nose in Würzburg on Anne Frankstrasse where the famed
Dutch-Jewish diarist hid hers *(that bump, illuminating Judaism's
central core)* in the attic. Still, today, whole families relax when
one's numbed, unable to feel pain when incisions are made—only
afterward: swelling, bruising around the eyes, unrecognizable.
Traveling for pleasure's a recent phenomenon for the Jew whose
midline projections depict a war theme, recalling heroes, libraries,
birthplaces, graves.

III
EVER PRESENT TENSE

Terza Rima or Traveling Forward While Looking Back

Rootless, Spanish moss filters
nitrogen out of air, draws
sulfur from rain, water vapor

from steam. Prompted to recall
her social, dates of death
and birth, I hunger for little

salt shakers, a Rummy Q set,
her Star of David in white gold.
I pay off her credit card debt,

gallop the last of her old
15 inch TVs to the dump.
There's no one left to go

home to, so I strum
this humid Georgia air,
still unused to *ma'am*

and *sir*, still prefer
a tea that's less than sweet.
I envy the moss hair,

the way it beards in heat
over others' branches.
I saved an old rug, a complete

cookware set, matched
sheets and comforters.
They say the plant's

"forgiving" because it grows
without anybody's help.
I disconnected her phone,

paid $9,000 for funeral
services, sold the car.
Garlanded like a coral

reef strung in trees, far
from its sea, I settle
like moss, bluish solitaire.

MOTHER LESS, MOTHER MORE

Mother Goose, Mother Guess
which Mother he'll love best:

Den Mother, Done Mother,
Fit Mother, Fat Mother,

Stepmother, Stop Mother
Hip Mother, Hot Mother,

Grandmother, Grind Mother,
Smother All the Time, Mother,

Motherlode, Motherland
Mother Bored by All She's planned,

Host Mother, Post Mother,
Modern-Slice-of-Toast-Mother,

Skip the Jokes and Roast Mother,
Pocket Full of Post-Its Mother,

Ring Around the Collar Mother,
Pinch a Penny Now, Mother,

Mother Speaking Motherese,
Mother, May I? Mother, Please:

scrambled easy, slice of cheese.
Find a Mother, pick her up,

& all the day you'll have a Cutlet,
Folded Laundry, Full Service, a Spa;

Mother Cheering, Mother Swearing
Sis-Boom-Bah! Mother see

as Mother do: Bad Mother,
Good Mother, Done the Best She Could

Mother. Now You See Her,
Now You Don't, and You Never Have

the One You Want.

After Reading a Letter from the Addict

She appears, loopy o's and dotted i's and *itsy bitsy*
teeny weenie from the front seat of the green station wagon,
bottles of lotions, heating pad and moans. From envelops she
spills like plastic tumblers stuffed into closed cupboards, multiplies
like dusty cans of cream of mushroom soup. There she is again:
she who means well, sings in the car, and buys too many cans, she
whose bathroom palace sorted medicines and creams, she with her
ice cubes and coatless winters, the heat of her *one-eyed, one-horned*
flying purple people eater. She reads Tom Clancy. She screams
at doctors, tucks me in, and says I can stay home because I'm
sick, we're all sick, she who conceives a house of witches must dance
in living rooms in underwear to Carole King, she who rests
under an eye pillow, who's never, *never*, to be disturbed—
she and I will sleep in, late, tomorrow.

Vicodin Poem #1

7% of patients who are prescribed narcotic or opioid
analgesics to treat chronic pain will become addicted
—National Institute on Drug Abuse.

"Missy, can you throw this out for me?"
Not a question but an order from our tired queen

of Hostess plastic wrappers. Not a foot
from the trash, I feel her in my nakedness,

my working robe today, calling her sister
to assemble our story like a toddler

puzzle with a few key pieces in the toilet.
Clumps of kitty litter, stolen grocery

cart under the laundry shoot, used
sofas and chairs, we inherit

the discarded. I don't remember vegetables
or manners, thinking now of my son

whom I've just delivered to another
caretaker's arms and the Azeri

proverb, "Not even a thousand aunts can replace
a mother." How I still seek their comfort,

how the Ngaka say, "When your mother

dies, you'll eat yam peels." How I baked,

melted butter; how I'd trade whole meals for her
numb, cold cans of white potatoes.

WORKSHOP ADVICE: TAKE THE GURU OUT

He's too hocus pocus for an American
poem. Orange cloth, brown flesh, another
continent enters the room when he's there,
part naked, crystal eyes, white
hair, encircled by women
who eat brewers yeast for breakfast. No, the guru

has to go. Too East, the peaceful guru,
a re-potted banana plant in American
soil. Choose a financial planner, a woman-
rabbi—anything but his bald patience smothering
the line. He hovers like a flock of white
birds over lovers on the coast, their

picnic lunch of fried chicken lying there
hopelessly exposed. Just the sound of it, "guru"
sounds too fru-fru, archaic, a white
lie for what you really want in American
art: Chinese take-out glare, sidewalk smothered
in butts, chewed gum. Hairy women

hang his picture by the birthing bed, women
who pray in private or chant their
musty breath in airport entourage; mothers
with babies in arms begging the dead guru
to bless them, inject India in American
souls. A replica swami hangs on white

walls in the ashram next to black and white

portraits: Mother Teresa, the only woman;
Martin Luther King, the only American.
His hippie dippie image belongs there,
not in your poem. Kudzu and gurus,
aurora borealis scarves and grandmothers—

big *no-no's*. Americans make ourselves other
holy figures: they're invisible or male and white.
Girl, here's our advice: lose the guru.

The paper sacks with fancy store logos,   their fragile
     handles, dented bodies,   tossed and carpeting,   suffocating
fast food wrappers, unwashed clothes,   needling   like   fire
ants,   their mounds sting   like her cross-   worded
     fuck-yous on refrigerator door posts,   her blood
               like chocolate syrup

          on kitchen   tile; it stuck   to our shoes;   we heard it
after   flushing the turtle's   murky water
which   smelled of death or   maybe
like pieces of skin she'd stuck to walls. *Artwork*, the notebook said—
Her body shrunk to collar bones,   pointy elbow pokes;
               her leg warmer

          summer;   decomposed   funk.
               Like when the earthquake   shook and the
plates shattered; the drawers pushed out from their chests like
beaten women. I didn't expect this   many needles. *At least*
we're all together, I said to my sober   sister,   my cracked
brother. We discarded   the   wallpaper   scabs,   filtered
               the tank's   substrate.

MOTHERS' APOLOGIA

After Yosef Komunyakaa

Please forgive me, ma'am,
for staring, getting involved

in your enormity,
it's my weakness to touch,

judge. You really shouldn't
sip coffee,

lug book bags or snack
on sugary cakes.

I was taken by an edge of exposed
belly, gourd-like breasts. Don't mind

if I touch you. Oh! I felt
paws! Fins! The sex?

The name? You won't
say? I'm moved by your privacy,

how you swallow your heartburn
with milk. Take no offense

from sideways glances—
How old are you, anyhow?

—That old?
Where else are you swelling?

Midwife? Birthing room?
Hospital? Epidural? Forceps?

Circumcision? Legitimate? Due date?
That late? By looking, I'd thought

farther along, younger, your second
or third. Have you figured out day care?

Your diaper brand,
changing table, glider,

breast pump, boppy, bouncy seat,
infant carrier, safety plugs,

mini-van, DVDs, pack-n-play.
I know it's none of my business, but

shouldn't you be sitting down?

VICODIN POEM #2: HOW SUFFERING GOES

I sit. The cramp spasms in calves and ankles.
The monkey mind scratches my mother's head
and her headache sharpens. The monkey laughs.
Her eardrum throbs where the monkey
pins his long pink finger and sticks out his tongue.

From the far right corner of the room someone sneezes.
A car engine, a cough. Needles prick my toes.
The Insight Meditation leader says to name your feelings.
Car rides with my mother: is that a feeling?
Naming and holding herself one part at a time.
Stomach stomach stomach and *neck neck neck.*

Two failed marriages, a childhood
of bandages. Self pity like a cool, wet rag pressed to her forehead.
The meditation leader says it's best to catch the pain early,
to come back to breath.

In the car with her I catch the pain early,
her beached body under afternoon blankets and bottles
of prescriptions willing to concede she's *sick sick sick.* The leader
says to name feelings three times before we scratch an itch, lift
a numb leg, or brush stray hairs from our face.

From the passenger side I say *pain* again and again. Still it's there
where *aversion* and *suffering* face me in the side-view mirror.
We climb stairs to Grandmother's apartment, and she cries
three times about her knees, her chant a haunt that echoes
from closets of old clothes, old minds,

old monkeys, always moving, scratching, knocking on glass.
They scream, their laughter, a group of girls running through
the apartment hallway. Rain falling over the porch. A change in light.
A small tremble of breath across the upper lip,
again again again.

When electricity went out because of *El Látigo*, The Whip, rains
that overflowed her low-lying room, she couldn't call home. Phone lines

down, she sat in the wet, mosquitoed courtyard for days.
When curbsides dried, an ant trail inched inside white wall clay,

crawled the wood floor to the sagging bed's heel and up
its crisp white sheets. On the bedside table, a close-up

of *la cara del niño*, a cricket marked on its face, an ugly child,
the devil's infant. These disease-burdened bugs with their wild

Mexican names, evenings of *swack* and blood on *la calle*
de las amebas, a street flood of intestinal worms and puffy eyes.

She was feeding someone Spanish in *psst psssts*,
tamale corn *masa* slapped between hands, balancing

the head's bread basket, cooking with cactus,
and *ay yay yay* became a song with silver buttoned pants.

Calling long distance the gringo refused the charges, asked her
to call back with an international plan. Love was far far away, there

and not there, like the mosquitoes' tinny ring.
She wanted to answer *¿Bueno?* Like a native, just beginning.

SHE WANTED HIM TO ARRIVE
LIKE A LONDON TRAIN

On a dirty concrete bench in a discarded city, warm
ice packs for feet, she wishes for an early baby, then

an on-time baby, then for a tired city bus to cough
its black exhaust halt at her stop. *When the West*

fails, go East, a fairy hip-momma whispered through clinks
of passenger change, so she made an appointment

to be rubbed by a Vietnamese foot swami then pinned
by an Anglo, scarf-headed woman practicing Japanese

medicine. The pricks woozied bloated insides.
She swallowed capsules of evening primrose, washed

sour drops of black cohosh down her throat,
rubbed her perineum, her breasts, her dog, the stinky

pair of flip flops that wobbled her past women in tailored,
tight-fitting suits, past shiny leather shoes,

and tall bodied, glass buildings. The nurse said envision
a thinning cervix; the yogi, blooming geraniums in the third

eye center. She focused on transit, swift glass doors,
blinking lights, a child's kicks and screams to get out.

Free Car Wash, Seven Months

Giddy fear of monstrous tongues
    licking the roof,

red-brush go-go dancers shimmying
    the trunk, car sides.

The wind tunnel skimming
    droplets of water, glossy

wet release into afternoon.
    Radiant, reborn,

even on cluttered backseat drives
    home to cracked asphalt,

weedy lawn of fallen crabapples.
    Once the conveyor

belts of my body deliver you
    from high pressure

pre-wash kicks and twists,
    of what, Child,

will you make your monsters
    and dancers,

having left my insides
    clean?

SLEEPING CONDITIONS

One new mother insisted on a king size bed
days after her baby was born. Another hushes
twins to sleep, girls by her side, husband

marooned in a room upstairs. A new mommy
hated her boy behind bars, but blushed,
said it was *that or her marriage*. In an economy

of sex and sleep, she tip-toed away for "visits
with baby." Teaching English in Laos four
years, my friend said they pitied her sitting

solitary in bed. At first, sisters came
to share sleep until she learned
enough language to say:

I prefer to sleep alone.
Privacy, a concept that didn't exist
in a village where abandoned munitions explode.

Western researchers find this incestuous,
mothers lying *dakine*, skin to skin until age
ten in Japan. Others claim the importance of touch,

a right not a risk, bald head at one's breast
the best possible way to sleep. I split
the difference, decide it's best

to spend some time apart. But by morning
I rescue him from the West,
to coo next to me, despite the warning.

Recalls Due to Violation
of Lead Paint Standard

Bright shiny words in shapes of soft sponge
boxes, roller coaster of words, looped
oranges, blues and greens, flashing light
words that say: touch me, tumble my plastic

boxes, a roller coaster of words looped
to burning gums, sucked cold ringing
words that say: touch me, tumble my plastic
lemons and frozen greens to toothless grins,

to burning gums, suck on my cold ringing
words recalled with words, colorless, flavorless
lemons and frozen greens to toothless grins
on a China boat where they manufactured more

words recalled with words, colorless, flavorless
in smoky cities, coughing on these cheap words
boated from China where they manufacture more
little toy ducks floating on sick seas, cautionary words

smoked from cities, coughing on these cheap words
soiling busy mommies who can't read words
printed on toy ducks, floating, sea-sick words
to the floor, liquidated words picked up

and eaten with his tiny, open, laughing mouth.
Oranges, blues and greens, flashing light
words to soothe and chill those sore gums, words to taste,
bright shiny words in the shape of a soft sponge.

I Dreamt Mung Bean

My student, Xuelai, describes this bean,
says it eases a baby's digestion. She sent pictures
of cow's bone, a delicacy served like a centerpiece,
brown cylinder standing on the plate
as if it had walked there on its own.
Pigs' feet, little paw cut into sixths, I learn
is a dish served to women to reduce
the wrinkle. In America, fat
reduces the wrinkle, so we eat bacon,
I tell her, tower over her in the cafeteria line.
If you eat brown rice and vegetables,
staring at fish eyeballs, things change.
My son is sleeping under the eyes of a stuffed
frog. It pleases me he sleeps. I check for the usual:
suffocation, rash, nose bleed, disappearance.
We're not often far apart from one another,
13th month "in the womb" and I wonder if I'll say
13th year, when his hair will exist in color,
uncombed, up to my breast, standing on his own.
My big strong cow's bone, I'll shout to him
when he's far outfield playing
our American sport, strong and lean
as our boys can be.

VICODIN POEM #3: AUGUST 1978

They say a woman forgets labor
once the baby's born, but Mother said
she never forgot.
She missed appointments with dentists, the counselor,
but she remembered to stop for soup, pour
canned broth into a bowl. She instructed
ice packs and ginger ale,
to wear basement slippers, and feel my way
around rusty nails.

Sour damp sickness,
loved with saltines and wet washrags.
For days, thermometer pressed to bed lamp,
I kept burning
like a rotten pear suffering openly
in a fruit bowl by the sill.

The handsome poet lamented his, compared it
to removing the clitorises of African girls, vaginas

dismembered or sewn shut for penises in full coats
of foreign skin. It was December and the cold

pounded on emergency doors wedged open
to night clouds of writers who smoked.

Would we all drop pants and call one another
the size and shape of genitalia? Swollen,

I carried 5 months of boy inside a sheer
purple blouse, the bruise of it, and the Star

of David pendant shining on its silver
chain. A mutilator, a Jew

who wished for a daughter, to be a good
daughter, to ask my circumcised husband to grip

our son's pink body strapped and screaming before
the cut. Jewish guests thought it best, they

who'd obeyed the same tact laws as 88%
of white, American men, whose sons

raced around a small island of celebratory
sandwiches, licking vanilla pastry from their mouths.

He'll return home
    once or twice a year with a batch
        of starlings and their new

undecorated heads
    followed by unrelenting
        talk of death, a mother's grey.

I look into relocation to Laos or Bhutan,
    anywhere children sleep with mothers
    until married.

Where a son doesn't leave parents in separate
    lonely houses, showering in private
    stalls with new pads

of shampoo on aging hands, humming
    songs to empty backseats,
        electronic greeting cards.

Bite me, I whisper to the sleeping
    giant-to-be in our shrinking
        morning bed. Press your foot

into the dry flesh of my thigh,
    claiming me before a whole set
    of big teeth takes over.

Sometimes I recline
in the fathers' chair, where arms
rest on wide leather, feet
propped. I order a drink,
hear the father in myself
who knows what he wants
and that someone is willing
to bring it. My fathers like
feeling important. They fiddle
with dials, check sprinklers,
and carry heavy ice chests
down porch stairs. They don't
judge their arms and legs, they
use them. My fathers aren't ashamed
of ample bodies. They wear them
in t-shirts from the St. Louis
Cardinals and Don't Mess
with Texas. My fathers would like
to be as large as Texas so they eat
man-sized cuts of meat. I find them
in summer at barbecues
or sauntering slowly around
picnic benches and talking
to willows. My fathers are not
afraid to be silent. Sometimes
they turn off the sound and still
watch the T.V. My fathers live
inside me, ask: how am I?
Could I use any help? When I strike

and miss they're there, bringing me
water. My fathers say
there's a next time. And because
they're so often right, I
believe them.

Scientists Work on 'Trauma Pill'
to Erase Bad Memories

Change O and Orange has no meaning
as a color, just range: palette, rainbow,
alphabet, sunrise to sunset without
fire. Remove any before moment—

rainbow colors arranged on a palette—
and you get no picture, just blue flowered
fire removing all that came before
the match. With a slow intentional burn

you get no picture, no blue flowery
hydrangeas, no paisley paper walls
matching slow intentions. Burn
your past and you lose the range, memory

of hydrangea colored paisley walls. Papers—
certificate, transcript, license, diploma—
you're past memory. Losses range
from black shoes to a grape dress. Take

a certificate, transcript, license, diploma
and drop their letters one by one:
lack shoes, rape dress. Take
what's broken and erase it

in your scalding bath. Rewrite
the alphabet. Without sunrise, sunset?
Persimmons, California poppies—if you
change O then orange has no meaning.

My Brother Who Doesn't Speak to Our Mother Comes to Visit

The rabbi says we never own our sons.
On loan these boys like never-ending books
whose stories ripen into skin and bone.

Fingernails bitten down, my brother
visits. Still jabbering about comic books
he once owned, lent to the rabbi's son

then lost. I used to mother him. Each one
of us now grown. My own son will look
to him for stories, plastic dinosaur bones,

to play a game of hearts, concentration,
or memory. The fledglings I mistook
as mine, the rabbi says I'll never own

but merely feed and clean between neck folds,
brush downy curls, turn ages like a yearbook
whose stories ripen into skin and bone.

No drips of breast milk once they're grown,
I tell myself as I feed my baby who hooks
his hands to mine. My little rabbi on loan,
into skin, his stories ripen, into bone.

AFTER THE UPS MAN SHOUTED "FEED YOUR BABY AT HOME" THROUGH HIS TRUCK WINDOW

—Beauford, North Carolina May 2007

Bionic Feeding Woman
whips breasts out, sprays
privacy netting over him,
through the window. She slays

public ignorance. Offensive,
angry and green, she stays
right where she is, extensive
superpower network plays

the news: Continental Airlines,
2003, Deborah Wolf charged
a terrorist during war time
for milky discharge

in the face of passenger
complaint; Toys R Us
September 2006, stranger
for a children's store to fuss

when Chelsi Meyerson
busted out her right to feed
in the store's corner, shunned
by five harassing employees

who called security. Cover-up!
Applebee's manager told
Brooke, mother of 8. Cover up!
insisted the United steward,

throwing a used blanket across
Alina and her baby Rose.
Captain Areola, Boob Boss,
Mutant Nipple, each goes

on nursing, fighting the disease
of propriety like diaper rash,
growing muscles, curing degrees
of fever with a stubborn milky cache.

FETAL PIG DISSECTION

Gender made it worse,
knifing incision points
through rows of nipples first.
Skin deep, we cut on black lab tables

along incision points, knifing
attention with high pitched squeals
at sight of skin. We cut class, lab tables
half full with the most dedicated boys'

attention to our high pitched squeals.
We begged to copy morning cafeteria notes,
half full with the most dedicated boys'
lessons. They handed over reproductive systems,

begging us to copy. In the morning cafeteria:
scrotal sacs, testis, sperm cells, penis, vas deferens.
Reproduction system lessons, hands
scribing taboos: ovaries, uterus, bladder, vagina.

Vast difference to say scrotum, testes, sperm, and penis
out loud. Who to ask to Fall Turnabout?
Reinscribe the taboo: vagina to penis, ovaries to testis.
Once a year we had to choose

who to ask to Fall Turnabout
in that formaldehyde room before scalpels sliced
the year. We had a choice:
untucked blouses, liquor in dark livers

like formaldehyde before scalpel slices.
November winds roughened by boys' hands
untucking our blouses. Dark liquors rivered
digestive systems, erectile tissues. Rumors sprouted

like new dandelions. Beyond bleachers
were rows of nipples. First
period, hogs tied for easy scissoring.
Gender made it worse.

The five year old boy hits helium
-filled metal balloons weighted by plastic clips-
sends each one skirting the cold grocery tile
past windows of dead fish, past my beaming
five month old son. The boy

never tires of bullying the balloon and my son
never tires of the show, hearty gut laughter
exploding from his tiny boy mouth.

    Punch the balloon,
    jump, laugh; punch
    the balloon, jump, laugh

and they go on until it's time
for mothers to pay for their eggs, milk,
and, in my case, a metallic balloon I hit
for a fizzled giggle on the stroller ride
home, for my son who falls asleep
after noon's excitement.

How smart Mother was.
Always guessing the words
before contestants. She sat
in her chair, mouth glazed
with cheap chocolates,
hand on a trashy novel.
I loved the shopping—enough
for a money clip, a trip
to Bermuda, a Corvette
wheeled on stage.
I'd watch my funny
mother and her suburban
nest of catalogs.
My mother, the winner, the shopper.
Mother was what Vanna
wasn't: smart, fat, graceless.
Had I been more like her
I might have guessed
the letters would
stop turning and bury
her showrooms on credit.
My mother, the puzzler,
my bankrupt muse,
I starved for her in that kitchen,
in front of the television
where she always won.

With two
small children
needs two
two sets of arms
hands reaching
tugging chocolate
new sweaters,
mine not even
mouths that mouth
wait just one
more minute
say *please,*
to be tickled
more time
tired, grasps
lives just beginning
and she is *just*
her age, self
bones, their teeth
She claims
like her husband's
less naked,
rusting except
of empty milk jug
spilled, spilled,

two small
children, a mother
two of everything,
arms, two sets of hands
reaching for a face,
fingers to new
nothing mine,
miserable mouths
one minute, one minute,
one more,
minute, *please*
and they do, begging
tickled one more
time and she tires,
for more of their lives,
they are *just beginning*
ending, just coloring
self echoed in fragile
teeth, *are mine, mine!*
their toes, hair
and she is sexless, sex
naked and rusting
a slice of them, a sliver
milk jug glass endlessly
spilled, spilled.

LESSON IN MODAL VERBS

I *can* use a phone, meaning that I am *able to,*
I have the ability to dial, to speak, to listen,

to be brief or extended as required
by economy and opportunity. This is a skill

unlisted on any resume but unmitigated, hedgeless,
like I *can* pick up the kids, put milk on a third shelf,

Swiffer wood floors, fold t-shirts by exact specifications.
In the South one *might could* remember Mothers' Day

before Mothers' Day and one *might could* shave
in a way that doesn't leave evidence of one's entire manly self

like a drought's ant invasion, or one *might could* tell the other
one has taken care of dinner, baby sitters, gifts for one's

mother. One uses *can* to talk about the present or future, abilities
achieved, such as one *can* breathe, one *can* take our daughter

to the bathroom before bedtime, one *can* run but one *can't* hide
from hypothetical pasts for which we employ *could*

as in I *could have* danced all night had you asked me which you *could
have* but didn't. Can I ask you a question?

You for whom English is second nature, you who should know better,
who could have asked for clarification, directions, who *would have*

if you had been me? Would you like to take lessons
in our language? Between pick up and drop off,

after snackbowls and bedtime stories, we can start
by studying requests and politeness conventions, move

to adverbs of manner followed by wishes and infinitives,
the verb phrase, to be, as in happily ever after.

And it doubles from corners,
flung into coffee

shops, multiplying
like cockroaches, cuffed

in cardboard, imprinted
on cushiony booths, copped

feels criss-crossing co-eds,
glotted human barks like coff-

ins, a showcase of muffins, clef
eruptions in vitamin C

need, germs rubbing off,
scoffing commands,

    "use a napkin,"
    "into your elbow,"

until he catches it,
barely a syllable,

stopped in a sleeve.

Not the dog kind, though canine-like after birth
    teats swelled, drooping like pendulous
    lips, perfectly rhymed with hooch: illicit
mound of flesh you'd

hide in a paper bag, this abandoned
    house, this loose skin curtain. Startling
    to be publicly reminded by a neighbor
asking, *when you due?*

as if this were a library book to return
    for a boyish figure with boobs
    like Miss-Yoga-Mat herself, front
porching, yapping about 200 pounds

after her own pups were born. *Took time,*
    she recalls as if this empty stem cell
    thrum were temporary, a Mylar balloon's
eventual neck leak, long past *cootchie coo*

and squishy peas. Loyal as the beach crowd
    pitching umbrellas, the pooch remains,
    digging holes, raising wet mounds
before the waves' flattening. Itchy and tired,

my children beg to go back, drive by the old,
    umbilical neighborhood, this pad
    of filler fat, buoyancy of life vest,
the past's relic, like Caesarion, Cleopatra's

first son, to whom we credit for early pooch
        labeling. Dog forums suggest spaying,
        rubbing Bitter Apple along the stomach
skin, longer fur. But I prefer long-waisted cotton,

night walking my second child down our block,
        watching a grown woman squirm
        over this stretch marked chamber
as if this bitch might bite.

FEMININE ENDING

In prosody, a line of verse having an unstressed and usually extrametrical
syllable at its end.

I think of Debra Winger carried off
the factory floor, muscle and brawn of desire,
workmates in catty backrooms, their hair
netted, one *tsk-tsk's* another, scoffs
at overbaked cookies, the treachery
of a mother painting her son's toenails pink.
Then think of the Spanish for hand, *la mano*, link
between *macha* article and fist, the very
grasp of it, bedrail moan, dramatic heart
monitors, anguish of what promises to end:
beast that burdens bladder, exhale knife
thrust and burn or barter your blood, start
the *push*! Again and again until the end
that never ends: *mid* and her suffix, *wife*.

NOTES

Section I "Imperfect Tense"—Takes information from years of research and teaching among communities of second language learners, most recently with adult North Americans studying Spanish in Mexico.

"Whorfian Hypothesis" –Coined by Benjamin Lee Whorf, refers to a theory in linguistics and anthropology that asserts one's language determines one's conception of the world. Italicized quote from Whorf's 1956 book, *Language, Thought and Reality*.

"When You're a Retired American Studying Spanish in Mexico and After Six Months Can Barely Order Something off a Menu" –Alludes to mistakes referenced by several North Americans I interviewed. "Estoy embarazada/o" is a "false cognate" mistake— "embarazado" appears like the English word "embarrassed" but really means "pregnant." Many learn "coger" means "to catch" (in Spain) but in South America *"coger un bus"* is "to fuck a bus." Another learner remembered a book-making workshop where her mispronunciation of the word for "pages" (*páginas*), led listeners to think she said "vaginas."

"Widowed NYC Teacher Studies Grammar in Mexico" –Based on several interviews with retired women who live semi-permanently or permanently in Mexico and find new forms of recovery and acceptance as older women. *"Te amaba, me amabas, nos amabamos"* means "I loved you, you (familiar) loved me, we loved each other" in the imperfect tense which emphasizes the enduring past. *"Siempre, con frequencia, a veces, todos los dias"* (always, frequently, at times, every day) —learners of Spanish are often encouraged to look for these tag words to help them decide to use the imperfect/enduring past versus the fixed past tense.

"First Grade" *–"tarea en español"*—means "Spanish homework."

"Frijolero Ex-Pats"— Takes inspiration from *The Bean Eaters* by Gwendolyn Brooks and Terrance Hayes' "Golden Shovel" form. *"Pan casero"* means home-made bread but to say something is made by hand you use "hecho a mano"—the fact that homonyms in English (e.g. "hand" for "hand-made and made by hand) are not the same in Spanish, often confuses adult language learners.

"In Mexico, Americans Struggle"—Some Americans that identify as "white" reported struggles with their racialization in Mexico— either looking like they couldn't possibly know Spanish or *"morena,"* darker skinned Americans who were often wrongly assumed to be native speakers. As with "Frijolero Ex-Pats" this poem highlights struggles with homonyms as well as issues of race, class, gender, and cultural norms.

"Iberian Chair 1840s, Decorative Arts Collection" –Takes inspiration from discussions with Carissa DiCindio at the Georgia Museum of Art.

"Kuo's First Attempt" –Takes inspiration from discussions with Kuo Zhang.

"Undocumented Youth March For In-State Tuition" –In March 2012 The Georgia State Senate voted to ban undocumented immigrant students from all public universities. Undocumented students from Georgia were already barred from the state's five most competitive schools and have been required to pay out-of-state tuition at other state schools.

"Mordechai Sheftall's Letter To His Mother, 1812" –Descendants of the Sheftall family, first Jewish colonists to Savannah in 1733, were also "the first to marry gentiles, the first to get baptized in the Methodist Church, and the first to bury in Colonial (vs. Jewish) Cemetery"--John McKay Sheftall's 2008 remarks to Mickve Israel's Congregation on the synagogue's 275th Anniversary. The Sheftall family bible is part of the Hargrett Rare Books and Manuscripts collection at the University of Georgia.

"1750, Natural History of Barbados in Ten Books"—The italicized text is from a book by this title shared with me by Anne Meyers DeVine at the Hargrett Rare Books and Manuscripts collection at the University of Georgia.

"1971 Traveler's Guide To Jewish Landmarks Of Europe" –Title of a book written by Bernard Postal and Samuel H. Abramson.

"Terza Rima or Travelling Forward While Looking Back" –Takes inspiration from discussions with Dr. Andrea Swiegart & Kevin Tarner in Plant Biology at the University of Georgia.

"Vicodin Poem #1" –Takes inspiration from Mineke Schipper's 2006 book *Never Marry a Woman with Big Feet: Women in Proverbs from around the World.*

"Mother's Apologia" –Takes inspiration from Yusef Komunyakaa's "I apologize for the Eyes in My Head: When in Rome—Apologia" which begins "Please forgive me, sir."

"After the UPS Man Shouted 'Feed Your Baby At Home' Through his Truck Window" – Inspired by several true incidents where nursing mothers were unjustly treated for breastfeeding infants in public spaces.

"Terrible Twos" –Takes inspiration from Anne Waldman's "Stereo" and Steinunn Thórarinsdóttir's "Horizons" sculptures.

ACKNOWLEDGMENTS

The author wishes to express grateful acknowledgement to the following publications in which some versions of these poems first appeared:

Alaska Quarterly Review: "Vicodin Poem #3: August 1978" (formerly "DesPlaines, Illinois 1978")
American Poetry Review: "Fathering"
Anthropology & Humanism: "Ghetto Teachers Apology"
Barrow Street: "She Wanted Him to Arrive Like a London Train"
Bellevue Literary Review: "Vicodin Poem #2: How Suffering Goes" and "After Reading a Letter from the Addict"
Best of the Bellevue Literary Review 2008: "Vicodin #2: How Suffering Goes" (formerly "How Suffering Goes")
Calyx Magazine: "My Brother Who Doesn't Speak to My Mother Comes to Visit"
The Cortland Review: "I Dreamt Mung Bean" and "Feminine Ending"
The Cream City Review: "Recalls Due to Violation of Lead Paint Standard"
Damselfly Press: "Scientists Work on Trauma Pill"
Dirty Napkin: "Mothers' Apologia"
English in Education: "Pinewood Estates Trailer Park"
English Journal: "Teaching Poetry in Georgia Schools"
Hampden-Sydney Review: "Georgia Horizontal"
Java Monkey Speaks: A Poetry Anthology: "My Brother Who Doesn't Speak to My Mother Comes to Visit"
Kritya: "Krakow"
Literary Mama: "Mother Less, Mother More"
The Mom Egg: "Sleeping Conditions" and "Lesson in Modal Verbs"
New Verse Daily: "You Receive a Present from Someone You Haven't Seen in a Long Time. Who's It from? What's Inside?" (formerly

"Who's It From? What's Inside?")

North Dakota Quarterly: "Dragon Fruit," Undocumented Youth
    March for In-State Tuition," "Dead Sea Vacation," "1971
    Traveler's Guide to Jewish Landmarks of Europe," "Two Moons
    Over Tel Aviv," "Woman Shows Me Where We Are in the
    Service," and "Kuo's First Attempt"

Pilgrimage Magazine: "A Taste of War"

Quarterly West: "Driving through North Philly"

Rio Grande Review: "Teaching Poetry in Georgia Schools"

Split this Rock Featured Poem: "After the UPS Man Shouted Feed
    Your Baby at Home"

Squaw Valley Review: "Woman Shows Me Where We Are in
    the Service"

Women's Review of Books: "Workshop Advice: Take the Guru Out"
    and "Cantor in Drag"

2017 Golden Shovel Anthology: Honoring Gwendolyn Brooks:
    "Frijolero Ex-Pats"

"My Brother Who Doesn't Speak to My Mother Comes to Visit" and
"Who's It From? What's Inside?" were nominated for a Pushcart prize.

"Women Shows Me Where We Are in the Service" was a finalist selected
by Gerald Stern for the Jewish Currents Poetry Prize and published in
The American Dream: A Jewish Currents Anthology.

The writing of these poems was aided by the following sources: a 2013-
2014 Fulbright, Oaxaca, Mexico; a grant from the Leeway Foundation
for the Arts; the Dorothy Sargent Rosenberg Foundation Prizes (2004,
2005, 2008) for Poets Under 40, the Waging Piece Poetry Prize, the
Anna Davidson Rosenberg prize for poetry on the Jewish experience,
and the Sarah Moss Award from the University of Georgia.

Gratitude also goes (in no particular order) to the following teachers, family, and friends for commenting on this book or its poems at various stages of development: Alicia Ostriker, Gerald Stern, Michael Waters, Anne Waldman, Paula McLain, Melissa Hotchkiss, Dorine Jenette, Stephen Corey, April Ossman, Latasha Hutchinson, the late Maxine Kumin, Students/Teachers enrolled in LLED 7710 & 8710 [Poetry for Creative Educators], Thomas Lux, Josina Guess, New England College MFA colleagues, creative anthropology friends, Alice Jennings, and the numerous frijoleros I met, interviewed and learned from in Oaxaca, Mexico.

Thank you to my family, whom I will always call home. Special thanks to my beloved husband, Jason Taylor, my helpmate and life partner, and for our children, Oren and Liya.

Melisa Cahnmann-Taylor has co-authored two books, *Teachers Act Up: Creating Multicultural Learning Communities Through Theater* and *Arts-Based Research in Education*. Her articles and poetry are about language learning, sustainable or fragile states of bilingualism, and teacher education. She judges the annual Anthropology & Humanism poetry contest and is the editor of the ethnographic poetry section.